# Perspective
## Devotional

# PERSPECTIVE

## DEVOTIONAL

**Charity Ritter**

ISBN: 978-1-936286-02-7

Scriptures taken from the Holy Bible, New International Version®, NIV®. Copyright © 1973, 1978, 1984, 2011 by Biblica, Inc.™ Used by permission of Zondervan. All rights reserved worldwide. www.zondervan.com The "NIV" and "New International Version" are trademarks registered in the United States Patent and Trademark Office by Biblica, Inc.™

Although the author is a mental health therapist, and her writing does incorporate valuable perspective from that career, she wrote this book not as a therapist, but as a friend and Christian author. No part of this book is meant to be a replacement for mental health treatment, nor is it considered official therapeutic advice.

Published by Discovery Gadget LLC
DiscoveryGadget.com

 DISCOVERY GADGET

# TABLE OF CONTENTS

# Introduction

Life is complicated. There are challenges and opportunities, traumas and joys, successes and failures, losses and blessings. Our lives are not always balanced. Some of us have more trials and hardships than other people. Some of us have seasons where all we can see are the challenges. When the troubles of this world get to feel heavy, we all have some degree of emotional and mental turmoil.

As a therapist, I have been blessed to work with those people who reach out for help during times of struggle. Now, in a different role as a Christian author, I have the blessing of writing about struggles to help those who are looking for a little encouragement. This devotional combines both passions in my life, to help those who are struggling and to write about our wonderful Creator.

I have learned through my life circumstances, and through my career in helping people with their emotional and mental health struggles, that an important factor that can turn a challenge into an opportunity, and a trauma into joy, and failure into success, and loss into blessing, is your perspective; the way you look at it. The Bible is the filter that we need to use to set our perspective. All things in life should be filtered through the truth of God's Word. That is where you will find opportunity, blessing, joy, and success.

Obviously, not every instance will be so blatantly turned positive. Some instances like the loss of a loved one, sickness, maltreatment, or trauma may not feel totally like a blessing. However, the Bible does tell us in Romans 8:

- If we can live with a mind centered on Christ, we will find freedom.
- Our suffering here on earth is not comparable to the glory of God that will be revealed to us.
- All things, even the terrible things that happen to us, can all work together for our good. What an amazing concept.

Most of us do not keep our eyes fixed on the truth of the Bible consistently enough to truly allow our perspective to see life in that way. The ways of this world so easily creep into our thinking. That is why getting a dose of Biblical truth daily is so important; it helps us with our perspective.

This devotional was written to provide the reader with a daily structure for better understanding God, themselves, and Biblical truths in order to better adjust to, and maintain, a Biblical perspective in their life situations. It is my hope that this devotional will help you with your emotional, relational, and mental health struggles. I encourage you to read through it chronologically, as some of the days build on those before them. The topics in this devotional are modeled after the book *Perspective: How the Power of a Biblical Perspective can Change your Life* by Charity Ritter.

# Day 1

## HEALTHY HABITS AND BALANCE

I have the blessing of helping people improve their mental health, something that we all need to do whether we know it or not. We are all looking for better health in some way or another. We want physical health, emotional health, relational health, and financial health. In fact, sometimes health even becomes an idol for some, making it seem more important than God is.

Some of us put in hard work everyday to care for our bodies through diet, nutrition, and exercise. Some of us put in regular hard work to care for our minds through counseling or support groups. Some of us have spent valuable time reassessing our financial lives, academic pursuits, and professional ventures. Some of us worry about our relationships and seek support or read books to learn to improve them. These are all wonderful examples of how to maintain a balanced and healthy life, and even the world agrees.

However, even the most healthy person, according to these standards, often misses another crucial part of their life in achieving good health: spirituality. Our spiritual health is by far the most important aspect of our lives, yet many of us fail to care for our spiritual health. The irony is that when we are spiritually healthy, many of the other pieces of life will fall into place. The stronger our relationship with the Lord, the easier it is to discern His direction and the more we will be on the right path in all the other areas of our life.

Have you ever had a puppy? When we got our puppy I had to train her how to take a walk. She would lay down in the grass every few feet, and I'd have to drag her along. As she got older and with the use of treats, we eventually learned how to run together. During one walk, it struck me that just as my puppy had to learn to walk with me, we have to learn to walk with the Lord. She had to keep her eyes on me to know where we were going. Instead of laying in the grass every few feet, she was now glancing back at me to make sure she was going the right way. If she would forget to look back, she would pull the leash to go off the path and I would need to pull hard on the leash to get her back on track. The more often she looked back at me, the less I had to forcefully pull her another way.

We do that, don't we? When we are not looking up to our Father in Heaven, we so easily begin to venture off the path He has for us, and things in life become unbalanced and unhealthy.

> Rejoice always, pray continually, give thanks in all circumstances; for this is God's will for you in Christ Jesus.
>
> (1 Thessalonians 5:16–18)

In order to stay spiritually healthy, we must spend time with God regularly. In fact, God invites us to pray without ceasing. In other words, we are to always be in communion with Him. This is most certainly easier said than done. Our American culture has us all running form place to place, trying to have as many experiences as we can, trying to make as much money as we can, and trying to get as much done as we can. But that is not the purpose of life—not even close. By pursuing what the world tells us to pursue, we will end up worn out, imbalanced, and stuck in negative habits, thinking, and feelings. Without a robust and healthy spiritual life, everything else in our lives begins to suffer.

Finding a balance in life is crucial for emotional and relational health. If you are too busy chasing after worldly things, you will start to feel that it sucks the life out of you. While on the other hand you can be busy all day with kingdom matters or even mundane tasks with a kingdom mindset. You will be able to be much more productive yet energized at the same time. For me, the days I wake up at 6am and spend time in prayer are the times when I have much more energy than the days I sleep in until 7:30am and get started right into the tasks of the day. I am able to ask God to prioritize my day, refresh my thinking. I can remember that the mundane tasks can bring glory to God as well, especially when I have the right attitude and allow God to prioritize what is most important.

> So whether you eat or drink or whatever you do, do it all for the glory of God.
>
> (1 Corinthians 10:31)

When we prioritize our spiritual health by spending time with God, reading scripture, praying, giving thanks, and enjoying His presence, we begin to enjoy God's heart. By tending to our spiritual lives, our emotional, physical, mental, and relational health improves, even things that seem to suck the life out of us can bring glory to God when we have the right focus. The topics of this devotional will aim at just that.

**Personal Reflection:**
- What does spending time with God look like for you?
- How can you create practices in your life that deepen your relationship with God?
- Is your life more reflective of the American culture than God's desire for you?
- What areas of your life seem out of balance? How might spiritual discipline help you to better balance your life?
- What tasks seem to suck life from you? How could you change your focus in those things?

**Prayer:**

Thank you for always being there. Help me to look up at you more so I can learn to walk more closely with you. I am sorry for neglecting my spiritual health at times. Help me to prioritize spending time with you. Help me to establish a richer, fuller, and deeper relationship with you. Give me a motivation to complete my tasks in a way that brings glory to you. Father, help me to work through this devotional with consistency and intention, even if that means waking up an hour early while the house is still quiet.

# Day 2

## Who Is God?

In the world we live in today, there are many different ideas about God. Your perspective on God is the foundation of your perspective on life. Some of us grew up knowing God and others have searched their whole life still feeling that they have not found God, or that God is just an abstract concept that cannot be understood. Some people have a strong faith and would surrender their lives in the name of the Lord, while others have concluded that there is no God at all.

If you are someone who is uncertain of who God is or if there is a God at all, the Bible is where you can find your answers.

The Bible offers many attributes of God. These attributes, some which are listed below, are descriptors of how God acts or how He moves through the world. Consider that as you read through some of the attributes of God.

God is the creator. He is our heavenly father. He is the provider of guidance, and He is accessible to us all. He is eternal, faithful, good, gracious, holy, immutable, impartial, just, loving, merciful, patient, perfect, righteous, sovereign, and wise. He is full of glory, and He is jealous. He is a person, a preserver, our provider, and our savior.

We can take away a few key points from this extraordinary list.

Jesus is both God and the Son of God. Jesus paid for your debt created by sin so you can have a relationship with Him.

For God so loved the world that he gave his one and only Son, that whoever believes in him shall not perish but have eternal life.

(John 3:16)

"I am the good shepherd. The good shepherd lays down his life for the sheep.

(John 10:11)

God is our comforter and protector. He will never let anything harm our eternal salvation through Him. Although God's protection does not mean that you will never suffer, it does mean that you will not suffer in vain. There can be a bigger purpose to your suffering if you allow God to redeem it.

Praise be to the God and Father of our Lord Jesus Christ, the Father of compassion and the God of all comfort, who comforts us in all our troubles, so that we can comfort those in any trouble with the comfort we ourselves receive from God.

(2 Corinthians 1:3–4)

And we know that in all things God works for the good of those who love him, who have been called according to his purpose.

(Romans 8:28)

We have access to the Holy Spirit to guide us and help us grow.

But the Advocate, the Holy Spirit, whom the Father will send in my name, will teach you all things and will remind you of everything I have said to you.

(John 14:26)

**Personal Reflection:**
- Have you accepted Jesus' free gift of salvation? How has this changed your perspective on life?
- Where in your life do you need to experience comfort today?
- What good could God be working toward in your circumstance?
- How does the Holy Spirit work in your life to remind you of God's promises?

**Prayer:**
Father God, I praise you for who you are. Help me to adopt a Biblical understanding of you and the difference you make in my life. I ask for your comfort and guidance in my life circumstances.

# Day 3

## Fear Of The Lord

Fearing the Lord is mentioned often throughout scripture. As a kid, I always thought it meant to be afraid of God because He could strike you down if He wanted. While He does have the power to strike you down, fearing the Lord does not mean you are afraid of God. Rather, it means that you have a reverence, respect and awe for God. Fear of the Lord is necessary to have a proper perspective of God.

If you fear the Lord, you give Him authority over your life, and you have respect for that authority and His commands. If you fear the Lord, you give God control of your life. One of the hardest things for many Christians to embrace is allowing Jesus to have complete control of their lives.

> And now, Israel, what does the Lord your God ask of you but to fear the Lord your God, to walk in obedience to him, to love him, to serve the Lord your God with all your heart and with all your soul,
>
> (Deuteronomy 10:12)

Fearing the Lord and giving Him control of your life means that you make His priorities your priorities and His plans your plans. The deeper your relationship with Jesus, the more you will experience peace, an indescribable joy, and an understanding that your life is His and your life's purpose is to serve Him.

> The fear of the Lord leads to life; then one rests content,
> untouched by trouble.
>
> (Proverbs 19:23)

Fearing the Lord, with a respect and love for Him, places you in His family. God is the father whose love for you is deeper that you can even comprehend. He is a loving Father, who knows what is best for you, is in control, brings you peace, and loves you with the compassion of a perfect Father.

> For as high as the heavens are above the earth, so great is
> his love for those who fear him; as far as the east is from
> the west, so far has he removed our transgressions from
> us. As a father has compassion on his children, so the Lord
> has compassion on those who fear him;
>
> (Psalms 103:11–13)

**Personal Reflection:**
- What is holding you back from fearing the Lord and giving Him authority over your life?
- What other gods are in your life today? What comforts do you put before your relationship with the Lord? Love of money? Vanity? Approval of Man?
- How has culture shaped your worldview in a way that cuts out a reverence and awe for God's majesty and authority?
- How might fearing the Lord be a blessing in your life?

- How can applying this to your life bring you freedom today?

**Prayer:**

Lord Jesus, Help me to place you as Lord over my life. Help me to see areas in my life that I am still trying to have control over. Show me how to surrender my life more fully to you.

# Day 4

## GOD'S LOVE FOR US

For those who find me find life and receive favor from the
Lord.

(Proverbs 8:35)

Jesus loves you. Some of us first heard these words as young
children, but the ability to embrace how much we are loved by
God is something that comes only as we deepen our relationship
with Him. Allowing that truth to sink down into your soul is powerful, and it brings with it miraculous healing.

You are loved by God, and you have a purpose that reaches
farther than you can see. God pursues you to be a part of His family. He loves you beyond what you can imagine. There are many
verses in the Bible that mention God's love of His children. The
extent of love and blessing that God has for believers is more than
we can imagine. But God does not love us just because we love
Him. Jesus came in love to pay the penalty for your sins first. The
Bible also tells us that He loves the world, all of us.

For God so loved the world that he gave his one and only
Son, that whoever believes in him shall not perish but
have eternal life.

(John 3:16)

Jesus loves you to the point of sacrificing His life to save yours. Jesus does not simply love you because you are part of the group identified as Christians. Jesus loves you personally, specifically and intimately. His love for you is uniquely for you. His love for you manifests itself in ways that speak specifically to your one-of-a-kind heart and soul.

> Are not five sparrows sold for two pennies? Yet not one of them is forgotten by God. 7 Indeed, the very hairs of your head are all numbered. Don't be afraid; you are worth more than many sparrows.
>
> (Luke 12:6–7)

He knows you inside and out, and He loves you. He knows every strand of hair on your head, and He loves all of you. You are loved. If you accept His gift of salvation, you are made perfect in God's sight, and you are redeemed.

**Personal Reflection:**
- Do you believe that God loves you personally?
- How has God shown His love for you in a unique or personal way?

**Prayer:**
Jesus, Thank you for loving me despite myself. Thank you for all you have done to redeem my life. Help me to live a life that more fully embraces and accepts your love for me.

# Day 5

## Who Am I?

Who are you? Consider your answer to the question. Now consider your answer to that question in light of introducing yourself to a new acquaintance. What about professionally, would you answer that question differently? How about in the deepest recesses of your soul—is your answer different? Regardless of how you answer that question, God has a lot to say about who you are. And God's truth about you should be the foundation of your perspective of yourself; how you define yourself.

> For you created my inmost being; you knit me together in my mother's womb. I praise you because I am fearfully and wonderfully made; your works are wonderful, I know that full well. My frame was not hidden from you when I was made in the secret place, when I was woven together in the depths of the earth. Your eyes saw my unformed body; all the days ordained for me were written in your book before one of them came to be.
>
> (Psalm 139:13–16)

For starters, you were created by God. Think about that—you are God's creation. When I make something, it is important to me. A piece of my creativity and care goes into making it. God in His majesty and perfection, created you. He created you with care for a purpose. You are His; you belong to God (Romans 14:8).

> The Spirit himself testifies with our spirit that we are God's children. Now if we are children, then we are heirs—heirs of God and co-heirs with Christ, if indeed we share in his sufferings in order that we may also share in his glory.
>
> (Romans 8:16–17)

You are a child of God, and as God's child, you are His heir through Christ Jesus. Taking that a step further, because you are an heir, you are royalty alongside Jesus.

In other words, when you accept and enter into a relationship with Jesus, you are adopted into a royal priesthood (1 Peter 2:9). That's not to say that you are powerful in and of yourself because of your royalty. Rather, you are royalty because of Christ's power in you. In fact, scripture goes on to explain that it is in our weakness that Christ's power is made perfect. So if you are one who focuses on your failures or your weaknesses, take joy in the knowing that your lack has the potential to bring great glory and honor to God. God knows your weakness and He has plans to use that for His purposes. That's the amazing power of God's grace!

> If we live, we live for the Lord; and if we die, we die for the Lord. So, whether we live or die, we belong to the Lord.
>
> (Romans 14:8)

> But you are a chosen people, a royal priesthood, a holy nation, God's special possession, that you may declare

the praises of him who called you out of darkness into his wonderful light.

(1 Peter 2:9)

But he said to me, "My grace is sufficient for you, for my power is made perfect in weakness." Therefore I will boast all the more gladly about my weaknesses, so that Christ's power may rest on me.

(2 Corinthians 12:9)

**Personal Reflection:**

- Who are you? List 5 truths about who the Bible says you are.

- After reading through these scriptures about who you are, do you struggle to believe any of them? If so, which ones? Why do you think you struggle to believe those truths?
- How have you seen Christ's power made perfect in your weakness?
- What weakness in your life can you release to God so that others might see God's glory through you?

**Prayer:**

Father God, Thank you that I am yours. Help me to release control of the areas of my life in which I am weak so that your power may shine more brightly. I am yours. Thank you for that grace.

# Day 6

## AN ETERNAL PERSPECTIVE

Have you ever experienced long hours or an extended period of time away from your home, and when you finally returned home, you were overcome by a renewed love for your place of residence? Or maybe you were away at college or living apart from your family for such a long time that when you returned to the house where you grew up, you experienced a deep sense of belonging that had been missing from your life? These sentiments contribute to the commonly used phrase: "There's no place like home."

Scripture tells us that we are not to live for this life, but rather we are to live for eternity, which is when we will finally be home with our creator.

> My Father's house has many rooms; if that were not so, would I have told you that I am going there to prepare a place for you? And if I go and prepare a place for you, I will come back and take you to be with me that you also may be where I am.
>
> (John 14:2–3)

> If we live, we live for the Lord; and if we die, we die for the Lord. So, whether we live or die, we belong to the Lord.
>
> (Romans 14:8)

We belong to the Lord. He is preparing a place for us. That is the life we are to be living for, not the temporary and perishable rewards of this life. Our purpose is to bring glory to God.

> I consider that our present sufferings are not worth comparing with the glory that will be revealed in us.
>
> (Romans 8:18)

When we consider our purpose and our eternal home, our perspective on life should begin to shift. Having an eternal perspective helps us to more fully understand our purpose. Part of our purpose is to share the gospel and prepare for eternity. We can start to see our circumstances, relationships, and suffering in light of something far greater than ourselves. We can find strength, comfort, and peace from our eternal promise, and we begin to see even the most difficult of trials with a fresh set of eyes. In this way, we can experience the highs and lows, the hills and the valleys, the good and the bad, with the ability to look past our circumstances—no matter what they are—and find opportunity to bring glory to God so that others might also experience eternity with Him.

**Personal Reflection:**
- What does it mean to have an eternal perspective?
- How can an eternal perspective change a thought, action, or behavior in your life today?
- What experience in your life might take on new meaning if you adopt an eternal perspective?
- How might an eternal perspective help to bring God glory and bring others to Jesus?

**Prayer:**

Father God, Thank you for the promise that we have an eternal home with you. Help me to adopt an eternal perspective so that my life might bring you glory and that others might come to know you.

# Day 7

## God's Purpose For Me

Having a proper perspective of our purpose in life has an amazing way of grounding us. It helps us to be able to better withstand the ups and downs of life. It gives more stability to our emotions in times of trial and hardship. Understanding and continuously reflecting on the purpose that God has for us can change the way you think, feel and function.

> "You are the salt of the earth. But if the salt loses its saltiness, how can it be made salty again? It is no longer good for anything, except to be thrown out and trampled underfoot. You are the light of the world. A town built on a hill cannot be hidden. Neither do people light a lamp and put it under a bowl. Instead they put it on its stand, and it gives light to everyone in the house. In the same way, let your light shine before others, that they may see your good deeds and glorify your Father in heaven.
>
> (Matthew 5:13–16)

We are created to reflect God and His kingdom in such a remarkable way that other people will know more about Him just by knowing and seeing us. We are to reflect God's image to the world. God has a purpose, and we all play a role in that purpose. God works through blessings and trials to teach us and mature us and allow us the opportunity to rely on His strength so that we can grow in our relationship with Him. The more that we do grow and live out of the maturity that comes in knowing the Lord more fully, the more other people will see the hope of Jesus and come to know Him

> And we know that in all things God works for the good of those who love him, who have been called according to his purpose.

(Romans 8:28)

I want to encourage you to allow the ups and downs in your life to strengthen you and grow you. Consider what it would look like to let the fear of the Lord override all other influences in your life. If you have a heart that longs to honor God, then let your thoughts, feelings, words, and actions reflect that.

Isaiah teaches us that we were created for God's glory. This is the highest purpose we could imagine.

Reflecting God and pointing to Him not only delights God, but it brings great delight into our own lives. Not to mention, it allows others to draw closer to Him because they see His goodness reflected in us.

**Personal Reflection:**
- What is your purpose, and what plans does God have for you?
- Would someone describe you as salt and light? Why or why not?
- How do your thoughts, feelings, words, and actions reflect

the Lord? In what area of your life do you need to invite the fear of the Lord to override the other life influences?

- How does your life bring glory to God?

**Prayer:**

Dear Lord, You created me on purpose with a purpose. You have set a path before me, according to your perfect and pleasing will. Help me to trust in you. Help me to live out the purpose you have set before me. Help me to rest in the delight of glorifying you and you alone.

# Day 8

## You Have An Enemy

The Bible makes it clear that we have a spiritual enemy.

Be alert and of sober mind. Your enemy the devil prowls
around like a roaring lion looking for someone to devour.

(1 Peter 5:8)

From the first to the last book of the Bible, we find consistent
evidence of an enemy that desires to destroy our lives, break our
fellowship with God, and create strife and tension in our relationships.

The thief comes only to steal and kill and destroy; I have
come that they may have life, and have it to the full.

(John 10:10)

Though the enemy is real, we often forget his existence, and instead, we spend a lot of time struggling against one another. While
it is true that people and their sin can cause us to suffer (and we can
also be the source of another's suffering), it is critical to remember
that God warns that our struggle is not with flesh and blood.

For our struggle is not against flesh and blood, but against
the rulers, against the authorities, against the powers of

this dark world and against the spiritual forces of evil in the heavenly realms.

(Ephesians 6:12)

Understanding this is crucial for us to have a Biblical perspective. Just knowing that you're under opposition can give you perspective on temptations, negative thinking, and even negative moods. God urges us to resist evil, pray against the devil's attacks, and flee from our enemy's temptations. When we shift our focus from the wrongdoing of another, and instead begin to focus on the spiritual battle, we allow God's Spirit to fight for us. Not only will this bring us peace, but ultimately it will deliver victory. After all, Jesus already won. The battle is His, and He remains victorious.

Submit yourselves, then, to God. Resist the devil, and he will flee from you.

(James 4:7)

The God of peace will soon crush Satan under your feet. The grace of our Lord Jesus be with you.

(Romans 16:20)

**Personal Reflection:**
- Do you have enemies? Have you ever considered that you have a spiritual enemy?
- How might your life be different if you blamed others less, and put more energy into resisting your spiritual enemy?

- According to James 4:7, how can you fight your spiritual enemy?
- Knowing that Jesus already conquered Satan and won the battle, how does that impact your fight against Satan's schemes for your life?

**Prayer:**

Father God, I confess that I spend a lot of time looking for people to blame for the pain, suffering, and struggles I encounter in my life. Help me to remember that Satan is the real enemy. Thank you for your Spirit, who remains on my side and fights for my life. Thank you for Jesus who sacrificed everything so that I might live in victory.

# Day 9

## SATAN'S ATTACKS

Having a perspective of spiritual warfare while going through struggles can be helpful. Though Satan does not know our thoughts (only God is omniscient), Satan uses our minds to attack us. Therefore we must use our minds to fight back. Often our thoughts and feelings of doubt, condemnation, accusation, and fear are actually lies from Satan that are infiltrating our minds. Satan lies to us to cause us to get off track and focus on the wrong thing.

When we face discontentment in the middle of the night or question our identity in the midst of a difficult situation, Satan very well might be at the root of those unsettling feelings. We cannot give them power by analyzing what they mean and asking if they are true about us, but rather we must stand firm in God's truths and only allow Him to define who we are.

> And lead us not into temptation, but deliver us from the evil one.'
>
> (Matthew 6:13)

In fact, the Bible instructs us to pray against the attacks of the evil one, and to use the truth of Scripture, given by God, to fight off Satan when he attacks.

In addition to all this, take up the shield of faith, with

which you can extinguish all the flaming arrows of the evil one.

(Ephesians 6:16)

Pray against the devil's attacks, and pray for others that they will grasp the truth, have faith in Jesus, embrace the peace of the gospel, and have a Christlike perspective. This will allow you and others to put on the armor of God and stand firm against our enemy.

Memorize Bible verses so that, just as Jesus did in Matthew 4:1–11, you can use Scripture to fight off Satan's temptations and attacks.

Then Jesus was led by the Spirit into the wilderness to be tempted by the devil. After fasting forty days and forty nights, he was hungry. The tempter came to him and said, "If you are the Son of God, tell these stones to become bread." Jesus answered, "It is written: 'Man shall not live on bread alone, but on every word that comes from the mouth of God.'"

(Matthew 4:1–4)

Finally, persevere through oppression with hope because the book of Romans explains that nothing can separate us from the love of Christ. Not even Satan's relentless attacks can separate us from Christ's eternal love. Spend quiet time focused on the Lord and resting in His Love for you. Allow Him to renew your perspective daily.

**Personal Reflection:**

- What lies from Satan does he use most often to attack you?
- What is one truth from God you can use to fight off Satan's attacks?
- How can you put on the armor of God?
- How can you use Scripture to fight Satan?

**Prayer:**

Lord, I need you. Only your words, your truths and your power can fight off Satan and his evil attacks on my mind, thoughts, and life. Help me to stand firm in you against the enemy.

# Day 10

## Sin

Our culture tries to skew our perspective on sin. We are told to do what feels right. What the world does not understand is that, although sin is in what separates us from God, Jesus' death bridges the gap caused by our sinfulness, and allows us to have a relationship with God. So as a Christian, admitting that you have sin issues does not mean that you will be rejected by God and punished.

For the wages of sin is death, but the gift of God is eternal life in Christ Jesus our Lord.

(Romans 6:23)

for all have sinned and fall short of the glory of God,

(Romans 3:23)

The Bible is clear about sin. Sin is anything that falls short of God's standards. Sometimes sin is unintentional, and sometimes it is intentional. We are born with a sinful nature that opposes obedience. When sin is intentional it is often because sinning is easier than obedience. We need Jesus to pay the penalty for our sin. He paid our debt for falling short of God's perfection, allowing us to live with Him for eternity. If you have accepted Jesus' free gift of salvation, you are now credited with Jesus' perfection in the sight of the Lord. Although we are credited that perfection, we still live with a sinful nature and will continue to fall short daily. But we are called to continually and humbly seek obedience to God, with a heart that is trying honor Jesus' sacrifice in the best way we can for today.

Romans 6:6 tells us that when we are saved we are no longer slaves to sin.

> For we know that our old self was crucified with him so that the body ruled by sin might be done away with, that we should no longer be slaves to sin—
>
> (Romans 6:6)

> The mind governed by the flesh is hostile to God; it does not submit to God's law, nor can it do so. Those who are in the realm of the flesh cannot please God.
>
> (Romans 8:7–8)

As long as we are on this earth we will continue to have a sinful nature and this makes it easier for Satan to tempt us into sin. That sinful nature—our flesh—is part of our human experience. However, if we have put our faith in Jesus as our Lord and Savior, we are saved by Jesus, and are no longer slaves to that flesh. We are no longer slaves to the sin in our lives, but it is still a battle.

Though sin is a part of life, those of us who are saved by Jesus have the Holy Spirit within us and have access to great power in battling sin. Seek Jesus, celebrate His gift of salvation, and lean on God's Spirit to help you live a life of obedience.

"Watch and pray so that you will not fall into temptation. The spirit is willing, but the flesh is weak."

(Matthew 26:41)

**Personal Reflection:**
- How does sin get in the way of God's plans for your life?
- How can you work to resist sinful patterns (selfishness, love of money, materialism, grumbling)?
- Describe a time when you were able to lean on God's Spirit and experience victory over your flesh's desire to sin.
- When you have overcome your flesh's desire to sin and acted in obedience, what emotions have you experienced as a result?

**Prayer:**

Jesus, Thank you for paying my debt. Because of you, not only do I get to experience eternal life, but I also have access to the power of the Holy Spirit in living a more obedient life. Lord, forgive me of my sins, and help me to live more obediently.

# Day 11

## GOD'S PROVISION

God provides. That simple two-word truth is packed full of promises, yet most of us struggle to live secure in that truth on a daily, hourly, and sometimes minute-by-minute basis. Understanding this truth is not simple but it can make a big impact on your perspective.

> And my God will meet all your needs according to the riches of his glory in Christ Jesus.
>
> (Philippians 4:19)

We all have times when the budget is tight, or we lose a safety net we previously had. Maybe you are afraid that your resources will not be enough to get you through the financial, professional, social, or emotional mountain before you. Sometimes God allows time of need or want in our lives so that we can come to Him in prayer as ask Him for help. He helps us to grow in our faith and reliance in Him in these times. Consider God's provision for Israel in Isaiah.

> For I am the Lord your God who takes hold of your right hand and says to you, Do not fear; I will help you.
>
> (Isaiah 41:13)

Time and again, He provides for our needs in surprising and unexpected ways. Not only does He provide for you financially, but you will continually meet His provision during difficult seasons that are stressful, overwhelming, and burdensome. When it feels like God is not providing, it is likely because you are not looking for Him. Maybe He wants to position you to make a change in your life. In ways that are specific to each situation and each person's heart, God will provide intimately, precisely, and graciously. Allowing this truth to influence your perspective will greatly reduce feelings of stress.

> The lions may grow weak and hungry, but those who seek the Lord lack no good thing.
>
> (Psalm 34:10)

> So do not worry, saying, 'What shall we eat?' or 'What shall we drink?' or 'What shall we wear?' For the pagans run after all these things, and your heavenly Father knows that you need them.
>
> (Matthew 6:31–32)

**Personal Reflection:**
- How has God provided for you financially in surprising and unexpected ways?
- Outside of finances, how has God provided for you?
- When your trust in God's provision is threatened, how do you typically grasp for control of the outcome?

- How has God provided for you in a way that was undeniably Him?
- In what area of your life do you most struggle with the truth and promise that God provides?
- How can you apply that truth and promise to that area of your life, and how might that change your perspective?
- If resources seem low, what change might God be leading you to? Are there things you need to cut out of your budget or life, or are there ways to find new resources? Seek after Him for guidance in your life.

**Prayer:**

Lord Jesus, You promise to meet all of my needs according to the riches of your glory. Thank you for knowing just what I need, even if what I need is a time of scarcity. Help me to learn in times of need that you are in control, and allow me to focus on my reliance on you and not myself or money. You promise me a life rich in your abundance, yet I still worry about so much. Forgive me, and help me to remember your truth and promise: You provide.

# Day 12

### Self-Image

For by the grace given me I say to every one of you: Do not think of yourself more highly than you ought, but rather think of yourself with sober judgment, in accordance with the faith God has distributed to each of you.

(Romans 12:3)

Our perspective: our thoughts and feelings about ourselves can impact our mood, our relationships, and our successes. We often focus on the negative things about ourselves, and sometimes we struggle with pride.

But he said to me, "My grace is sufficient for you, for my power is made perfect in weakness." Therefore I will boast all the more gladly about my weaknesses, so that Christ's power may rest on me.

(2 Corinthians 12:9)

Our weaknesses are a big part of who we are, and we must be aware of them to understand our need for Jesus. However, the Bible does not stop there in defining our identity. You cannot get stuck only on your negatives. You must acknowledge your weaknesses with the perspective that you are a work in progress.

being confident of this, that he who began a good work in you will carry it on to completion until the day of Christ Jesus.

(Philippians 1:6)

Remind yourself daily how much God loves you and that He has chosen you for a purpose in His kingdom, even if you do not fully understand what that purpose is quite yet.

See what great love the Father has lavished on us, that we should be called children of God! And that is what we are! The reason the world does not know us is that it did not know him. Dear friends, now we are children of God, and what we will be has not yet been made known. But we know that when Christ appears, we shall be like him, for we shall see him as he is.

(1 John 3:1–2)

**Personal Reflection:**
- What negative thoughts do you repeat about yourself when you feel overloaded or overwhelmed?
- Use those negative thoughts about yourself to fill out the following chart: (Refer back to Day 5 "Who Am I?" for Biblical truths.)

Negative Thoughts:

-

-

-

Biblical Truth:

-

-

-

Who I Am:

-

-

-

What is your main takeaway from this exercise?

What will you do to remind yourself of how God sees you everyday? (Ideas: Bible verses on sticky notes, daily worship songs, daily prayer, accountability groups, online teachings, words of encouragement on your mirror, etc.)

> Finally, brothers and sisters, whatever is true, whatever is noble, whatever is right, whatever is pure, whatever is lovely, whatever is admirable—if anything is excellent or praiseworthy—think about such things.
>
> (Philippians 4:8)

**Prayer:**

Father God, Thank you for the people in my life. Thank you for the opportunities you have given me. Please change my judgmental attitude, and help me to see the plank in my own eye. Fill me with the love and grace that can only come from you so that others will see your light shining through me.

# Day 13

## PRIDE

Pride is a vicious trap. It's also a trap into which we can easily fall. Pride skews our perspective. Our culture defines pride as a confidence or satisfaction gained from one's own achievements. On the surface this doesn't seem as if it would be sinful. However, it is very easy to forget God's role in empowering you to accomplish anything at all. It's easy to forget that all of life is because of God, and therefore it's easy for us to take credit for our noted accomplishments and achievements. This is a slippery slope, often leading us to putting ourselves before others and even before God. When we prefer our will over God's, pride is at work in us.

> In his pride the wicked man does not seek him; in all his thoughts there is no room for God.
>
> (Psalms 10:4)

> But when his heart became arrogant and hardened with pride, he was deposed from his royal throne and stripped of his glory.
>
> (Daniel 5:20)

The antidote to pride is humility. Humility is not thinking of ourselves poorly, but rather thinking less of ourselves. We should be aware of the strengths that God has given us and the talents and calling He has placed in our lives. Knowing our value to God is crucial, but humility allows us to understand how valuable we are while knowing how valuable others are as well. Humility allows us to put others before ourselves just as Jesus put Himself before us when He died on the cross for our sins. One way for us to live with greater humility is to consider others before ourselves in a way that we are willing to sacrifice for the other person. When we shift our focus from ourselves and place our focus on others, we begin to posture ourselves more humbly before others and God.

> Do nothing out of selfish ambition or vain conceit. Rather, in humility value others above yourselves, not looking to your own interests but each of you to the interests of the others.
>
> (Philippians 2:3–4)

> Where there is strife, there is pride, but wisdom is found in those who take advice.
>
> (Proverbs 13:10)

> Live in harmony with one another. Do not be proud, but be willing to associate with people of low position. Do not be conceited.
>
> (Romans 12:16)

**Personal Reflection:**

- In what areas of your life are you most prideful?
- How has pride prevented you from experiencing God's will for your life?
- What is one thing you can do today to live with greater humility?
- How does humility lead you to harmony with others?
- How does humility glorify God?

**Prayer:**

Lord, Forgive me for my pride. Help me to think less of myself and more of you and others. Lead me in humility, and help me to know when my pride has gotten in the way of me living in harmony with others. Help me to live with more of you and less of me.

# Day 14

## ATTITUDE

Our attitude is the external expression of our perspective. It is so easy to have a bad attitude, to complain, to grumble, and to think you have a better understanding of something than someone else. But those who are followers of God are to be content even in times that are not favorable to them. We are to have an attitude that brings glory to God, even in difficult times. In doing so, we focus on the joy that we have in Christ rather than seeking joy only through favorable circumstances. When we struggle with our attitude, it is a direct signal that there is a problem in our perspective; the way we think and understand life.

When should find joy in Christ despite our circumstances, we shine like stars in the sky. This is our witness to others. When we shine, we reflect the goodness of God and the joy of Jesus.

> Do everything without grumbling or arguing, so that you may become blameless and pure, "children of God without fault in a warped and crooked generation." Then you will shine among them like stars in the sky
>
> (Philippians 2:14–15)

This shift in attitude is attainable when we keep a Biblical perspective, remembering that this world is not our home. We are living for eternity not for today, and God has a purpose in all things.

Keeping this perspective allows God's peace to transcend the ways of this world. When the world wants us to believe that things could not be worse, the truth of Jesus protects our hearts and minds, and we can know God's transcending peace.

> And the peace of God, which transcends all understanding, will guard your hearts and your minds in Christ Jesus.
> (Philippians 4:7)

This is not to say that we are to put on a happy face regardless of our circumstances. Not at all! God gifted us with a full range of emotions. Because of God's Spirit living inside of those who are saved, we can know peace, comfort, contentment, and even joy in the face of difficulty. God is a God of both-and. We can carry our need, grief, sadness, and emotions at the same time that we can experience God's peace, comfort, love, and joy. This is evidence of the wonderful, mighty, and miraculous power of God!

**Personal Reflection:**

- In what area of your life are you most tempted to grumble and complain?
- Would others describe you as someone with a negative or positive attitude? Why or why not?
- Describe a time when you experienced God's peace despite the difficult circumstances surrounding you?
- Describe a time when you felt God sharing in your sadness or grief? Did that also bring you peace and comfort?
- How can you seek the joy of Jesus in the midst of pain?

**Prayer:**

God, I need you. Only by your Spirit can I have a positive attitude in the midst of this hurting world. Forgive me for grumbling and complaining, and help me to discover your peace, comfort, contentment, and joy in all circumstances. Help me to continue to develop a Biblical perspective and keep your truths at the forefront of my mind. Thank you for all you have done for me and help me to remember my blessing and my purpose here on earth.

# Day 15

**SUFFERING**

What role has suffering played in your life? The perspective we have on suffering is the difference between a blessed life or growing bitter and depressed. Some are born into suffering while others experience moments of suffering sporadically throughout their lives. Many endure seasons of hardship while some encounter deeply traumatic circumstances. Regardless of the suffering you have faced, God will bring blessing and purpose in it.

Let us then approach God's throne of grace with confidence, so that we may receive mercy and find grace to help us in our time of need.

(Hebrews 4:16)

God is our refuge and strength, an ever-present help in trouble.

(Psalm 46:1)

God allows our suffering to soften us toward Him. When we go to Him in our suffering, we discover a richer, fuller, and more loving and compassionate God than we previously knew. We discover a God who hears us, a God who grieves alongside us, and a God who comforts us.

And we know that in all things God works for the good of those who love him, who have been called according to his purpose.

(Romans 8:28)

God will bring purpose to our suffering. Whether it be in the mundane tasks of our lives or the deeply painful moments, God has a bigger plan. Whether His plans can be deciphered or remain unseen, God is faithful to His promises and He is piecing together all the parts of your life to mold you into the person that He made you to be. He has a purpose in the blessings and in the hardships. He has a purpose in prosperity and in need. To fully embrace a God-given peace, to fully trust in God's plans for our lives, and to fully grasp God's sovereignty, we must turn to His Word.

And the God of all grace, who called you to his eternal glory in Christ, after you have suffered a little while, will himself restore you and make you strong, firm and steadfast.

(1 Peter 5:10)

The Bible promises an end to suffering. Whether your relief comes in this life or after you have met the Lord for yourself after death, suffering will not last forever. Suffering in this life provides us with an intimate experience of Christ because He too suffered. We will experience a strength and supernatural peace that only comes from our savior who also suffered. In that, He shares in our suffering, and by His grace, we can share in His glory.

Now if we are children, then we are heirs—heirs of God and co-heirs with Christ, if indeed we share in his sufferings in order that we may also share in his glory.

(Romans 8:17)

**Personal Reflection:**
- How has suffering drawn you closer or farther away from God?
- In what ways has God carried you in your suffering?
- What have you learned about yourself and about God as a result of your suffering?
- What might it look like for you to seek God the next time you endure pain, hardship, or suffering?

**Prayer:**
God, Thank you for sending Jesus to suffer and die so that our suffering can have purpose. Thank you for carrying me throughout the pain, difficulty, sadness, and heartache I have endured in my life. Show me how to draw closer to you especially when the world grows dark around me. I need you. Help me to keep my eyes fixed on you in my suffering so that I can embrace your plans and purposes even in times of suffering.

# Day 16

## OTHERS FIRST
## (NOT TAKING OFFENSE)

To be human and sinful is to be selfish. No matter how hard we try, we are inevitably going to move through the world with a desire to please ourselves. As if that wasn't enough, our Americanized culture sends the messages: "Look out for yourself, do what feels right, and take control of your life." These messages fuel our already self-obsessed wants, needs, and desires. But this is not the way of Jesus.

Those who love and follow Christ are to follow His example. He sacrificed His right, His safety, and His basic needs—all of it He sacrificed for us. As followers of Christ, we are to be focused on others, putting others' needs before our own. We are to live humbly, sacrificially, and selflessly for the sake of others coming to know Jesus. Consider how this direction to put others before ourselves is given in Philippians.

Do nothing out of selfish ambition or vain conceit. Rather, in humility value others above yourselves, not looking to your own interests but each of you to the interests of the others.

(Philippians 2:3–4)

Be completely humble and gentle; be patient, bearing with one another in love. Make every effort to keep the unity of the Spirit through the bond of peace.

(Ephesians 4:2–3)

Coupled with this is the way in which we encounter people and circumstances that offend us. It's impossible to move through life without experiencing words from another person or a situation that contradicts our opinions, ideals, or preferences. However this is part of the economy of life. In fact, Jesus told us that we will experience trouble in this world. He said:

"I have told you these things, so that in me you may have peace. In this world you will have trouble. But take heart! I have overcome the world."

(John 16:33)

Do not pay attention to every word people say, or you may hear your servant cursing you—for you know in your heart that many times you yourself have cursed others.

(Ecclesiastes 7:21–22)

In essence, the things in life that offend us are not an excuse for us to lack in love, grace, mercy, and forgiveness toward others. Even in the most offensive of situations, we are still to seek Jesus, for He knows better than anyone what it demands of us to love selflessly and sacrificially despite being offended.

**Personal Reflection:**

- What does it look like to live selflessly and sacrificially in this culture?
- What offends you? How do you respond or react when you have been offended?
- What role does forgiveness play in living a life that puts others before yourself?
- How can focusing on Jesus' sacrifice help you the next time you are offended?

**Prayer:**

Lord, Forgive me for living so selfishly. Only by your grace can I live a life that puts others before myself. Guide me and lead me in living humbly, sacrificially, and selflessly. Help me to keep your sacrifice in the center of my thoughts so that I can sacrifice my wants and needs for others in a way that honors you.

# Day 17

## REJECTION

Can you remember a time that you experienced rejection? Maybe you have a childhood memory of being picked last for a team, or maybe you have been rejected by a romantic interest. Maybe your experience with rejection runs deeper, such as a father who left or a spouse who walked out on you. Rejection can be deeply painful. The fear of being rejected is something many of us struggle with in some capacity. Many of us are driven by that fear, creating entire lives that attempt to buffer and protect us from rejection. More subtly, many of us make decisions from a desire to please others, or a fear of being rejected.

However, if you engage in a relationship with Jesus, you are promised to never face rejection by Him. Jesus will never reject you. Though the world, and possibly even other Christ-followers, can and will reject you, Jesus never will.

Greater love has no one than this: to lay down one's life for one's friends. You are my friends if you do what I command. I no longer call you servants, because a servant does not know his master's business. Instead, I have called you friends, for everything that I learned from my Father I have made known to you. You did not choose me, but I chose you and appointed you so that you might go and bear fruit—fruit that will last—and so that whatever you ask in my name the Father will give you. This is my command: Love each other. "If the world hates you, keep in mind that it hated me first. If you belonged to the world, it would love you as its own. As it is, you do not belong to the world, but I have chosen you out of the world. That is why the world hates you.

(John 15:13–19)

Though it's easier said than done, we should not live lives afraid of rejection. The Bible tells us that rejection is part of the Christian life. The world rejected Christ, and the world will reject you as a follower of Him. But you can be confident in this: the commitment He has to you because of Christ can never be broken.

Consider these truths, and ask God to help you shift your focus from pleasing man to seeking and pleasing God, and God alone. Keeping this in proper perspective can allow you to live a richer, more authentic Christ-centered life.

**Personal Reflection:**
- Describe a time that you experienced rejection. How did that experience shape your future?
- Do you consider yourself a people-pleaser? Why or why not?
- How might your life be different if you fully embrace the promise that Jesus will never reject you?
- What truth from God do you need to hold onto today in an effort to live less afraid of rejection?
- What in your life would be different if you lived to serve the Lord without fear of rejection?

**Prayer:**

Lord God, Thank you for the incredible gift of your unwavering commitment to me. Thank you for graciously sticking with me at all costs. Help me to live less afraid of rejection, and help me to stop living with a concern for pleasing others. I want to live for you and for you alone.

# Day 18

## HYPOCRISY

We can all be hypocritical to some degree. When we measure others or ourselves against another, we essentially create a system by which to measure others and ourselves. Even the simple and passing thought of a person's appearance is relative to something—usually some arbitrary standard we've created within our own mind.

> "Do not judge, or you too will be judged. For in the same way you judge others, you will be judged, and with the measure you use, it will be measured to you.
>
> (Matthew 7:1–2)

> But the Lord said to Samuel, "Do not consider his appearance or his height, for I have rejected him. The Lord does not look at the things people look at. People look at the outward appearance, but the Lord looks at the heart."
>
> (1 Samuel 16:7)

As followers of Christ, we are to build others up and extend them grace. If we can change the way we think about others and ourselves to involve more compassion and acceptance of others, our hypocrisy will begin to lessen. By having a compassionate and accepting perspective of others and ourselves, we can free ourselves from whatever arbitrary measure we have used on others. We need to intentionally change our thinking, shifting our focus from measuring others by worldly standards and outward appearances. Instead, we need to adopt the measure that God uses—a measure of one's heart.

> Do not let any unwholesome talk come out of your mouths,
> but only what is helpful for building others up according
> to their needs, that it may benefit those who listen.
>
> (Ephesians 4:29)

> You hypocrite, first take the plank out of your own eye,
> and then you will see clearly to remove the speck from
> your brother's eye.
>
> (Matthew 7:5)

**Personal Reflection:**
- By what grounds or measures do you see others? (The clothes they wear? The company they keep? The cleanliness of their home? Their finances? Their vocabulary or speech?)
- In times of stress, do you ever find yourself striving to meet that impossible measure as well?
- In what areas do you look down on and condemn others, all the while ignoring your own struggles?
- In what ways do you need to give more grace to others?

- How have the corrupting words of another affected you?
- What difference would it make in your life if, instead of those corrupting words, others shared words with you that built you up?
- In what circumstances do you need to watch what you are saying in order to build others up instead of tearing them down?
- A hypocritical attitude is something that we all struggle with from time to time. Pay attention to your thoughts and the words that you say. Practice praising God for people in your life even when they do not meet your expectations.

**Prayer:**

Father God, Thank you for the people in my life. Thank you for the opportunities you have given me. Please change my hypocritical attitudes and help me to see the plank in my own eye. Fill me with a love and grace for others that can only come from you so that others will see your light shining through me.

# Day 19

## STRONGHOLDS

Psychology talks about core beliefs, which are beliefs that we hold determining how we perceive and interpret the world. There is an entire psychotherapy model built around changing these, because they are most often not true at all. The Bible calls these strongholds and tells us how they are handled.

> For though we live in the world, we do not wage war as the world does. The weapons we fight with are not the weapons of the world. On the contrary, they have divine power to demolish strongholds. We demolish arguments and every pretension that sets itself up against the knowledge of God, and we take captive every thought to make it obedient to Christ.
>
> (2 Corinthians 10:3–5)

We are in a spiritual battle, and Satan is our opponent. Satan is the father of lies, and when we believe his lies, they can become strongholds in our lives. Strongholds are lies that we have believed that run deep into the way we have defined ourselves and the world around us. These lies are well defended by skewed human logic that we have built, and used to try to explain the world around us.

If you are battling something in your life that does not seem to budge, it may be a hidden stronghold. If you have an unhealthy line of thinking that does not want to change even though you are trying to fight it, you may have to dig deeper and ask the Lord to reveal to you what stronghold that is hidden.

Strongholds can be thoughts such as, "everyone is against me," "I am worthless," "other people are stupid," "I can't trust anyone," "everyone is out for themselves," "I am going to make the wrong decision," and many more. The Word of God is the weapon against these lies. Jesus used the Word of God in Matthew 4 when He was in the wilderness. If you use God's Word to demolish strongholds, it will improve your thinking, your feelings, and your functioning. It will change your perception and your interpretation of the world, your purpose, and God. It will change your life. Jesus set us free from sin, yet when we continue to allow a wrong way of thinking (a stronghold), we'll struggle to experience that freedom throughout our lives.

**Personal Reflection:**
- What thoughts do you often hear in your head that might be strongholds?
- What does the Bible say about those thoughts?
- Are those things true according to God's Word?

Using the following chart, how can you use Biblical truth against strongholds?

Strongholds:
- 
- 
- 
-

Biblical Truths:

-

-

-

-

New thoughts:

-

-

-

-

**Prayer:**

Lord Jesus, Thank you for setting us free from sin and sinful thought patterns. Help me to identify the lies from Satan that I have allowed to imprison me through an untrue way of thinking. Help me to remember your truth and live in the freedom with which you have blessed me.

# Day 20

## Fear

Fear is the driver of so many of our choices and decisions. If you lived through the 2020 global pandemic, and you probably did, you likely experienced varying levels of fear. Depending on what you feared and to what degree, you either wore a mask or didn't, went to the grocery store or had groceries delivered, physically interacted with family members or social distanced, or some variation of these things. Even if your choices were based on data, health, and safety, fear likely played some role in your decision-making as well.

The pandemic aside, fear manifests in many aspects of our lives: work, relationships, family, lifestyle, health, and hobbies, just to name a few. For some of us, fear is paralyzing. One fearful thought and we are stopped in our tracks, unable to continue on. Others of us are often described as fearless and either don't even have many fearful thoughts or have them and ignore them. No matter our fear, or lack thereof, God gives us an antidote to fear: Love.

God's love casts out all fear (1 John 4:18). This may just seem like a nice sentiment, but it can be hard to grasp the practicality. To allow God's love to cast out the fear we carry with us into a situation, we have to keep a proper perspective of our purpose in this world and God's love, care, and plans for us. When we embrace God's sovereignty, omniscience (all-knowing), omnipotence (all-powerful), and His constant, promised, and faithful love, we can live a life less riddled by fear and more infused with faith and peace.

> Peace I leave with you; my peace I give you. I do not give to you as the world gives. Do not let your hearts be troubled and do not be afraid.
>
> (John 14:27)

Having a proper perspective of God's love and your circumstances as a way to grow in your reliance of God is the antidote for fear. It's helpful to remember, God has overcome the world. There is not a single aspect of this life that God isn't sovereign over. God is eternal, and His eternal presence is completely and utterly in control of everything. When life is hard and uncertain, seek the love of an eternal and sovereign God, and allow Him to melt away your fear.

**Personal Reflection:**
- What role does fear play in your life?
- How can you embrace God's love in the midst of your fear?
- How might your life be different if you seek God's love in the face of fear?

**Prayer:**
Lord God, Your love has greater power than anything I could ever imagine. Surround me in your love, especially during those times that I am most afraid. Help me to seek you and find you when I am living in fear.

# Day 21

## GOD'S LOVE IN YOUR TRIALS

One of the most important but hardest times to hold on to a proper perspective in life is while we are facing trials. Sadly, many Christians live with a false idea that the Christian life should be an easy life. Nothing could be farther from the truth. While a Christian life should be one full of joy, peace, and love, it's not a fast pass to easy street.

Truly my soul finds rest in God; my salvation comes from him. Truly he is my rock and my salvation; he is my fortress, I will never be shaken.

(Psalm 62:1–2)

The name of the Lord is a fortified tower; the righteous run to it and are safe.

(Proverbs 18:10)

Christianity is not a pathway toward comfort and happiness. Rather Christianity is an invitation to experience the truest and most pure source of joy, peace, grace, mercy, and love amidst an often difficult and uncomfortable life. 1 Peter describes how we are to process difficulty.

Dear friends, do not be surprised at the fiery ordeal that has come on you to test you, as though something strange were happening to you. But rejoice inasmuch as you participate in the sufferings of Christ, so that you may be overjoyed when his glory is revealed.

(1 Peter 4:12–13)

The Bible tells us that we will have trials and suffering in this life, but God will be our strength. He will make something beautiful out of the trials that we endure. Our flesh will want to run, hide, or control our trials in an effort to avoid pain; however, in order for God to make something out of our trials, we must draw close to Him. By doing so, we allow Him to strengthen our hearts through the trials we endure.

Blessed is the one who perseveres under trial because, having stood the test, that person will receive the crown of life that the Lord has promised to those who love him. When tempted, no one should say, "God is tempting me." For God cannot be tempted by evil, nor does he tempt anyone; but each person is tempted when they are dragged away by their own evil desire and enticed. Then, after desire has conceived, it gives birth to sin; and sin, when it is full-grown, gives birth to death.

(James 1:12–15)

Friend, please know that God is with you in the midst of trials. He is not absent in the times when you cry out to Him in pain and exhaustion. He strengthens you from within as you lean on

Him. He is not absent in those quiet times when you do not feel Him close to you. He does some of His most profound work when we cannot see what He is doing. When you think He is not doing anything, He is behind the scenes working out details that you wouldn't even have thought to consider. God is faithful and trustworthy, and He is always with you. It is important to keep pressing into Him, and in time, you will see His work and feel His comfort.

**Personal Reflection:**
- How has your faith helped you to endure the trials in your life?
- Did you seek God, Jesus, faith, or the church as a means to an easier life? If so, have you been able to shift your perspective? Why or why not?
- What have you learned about yourself and God as a result of the trials in your life?
- What trails are you facing today? What can you learn from them?
- What can you do today to take one more step toward relying on God to get through your trial?

**Prayer:**
Father God, life is hard. Thank you for your love, consistency, and dependability amidst the difficulties in my life. Thank you that you are sovereign over all things. Help me to seek you in all things and even in my darkest moments. Help me to see you working and feel your comfort in the trials that I am facing today. Thank you for remaining faithful to me even when I doubt.

# Day 22

## CAST YOUR ANXIETY ON THE LORD

Anxiety is the worry about everyday situations. Anxiety might manifest in our parenting, our finances, our relationships, our jobs, and our communities, among just about every other area of life. Sometimes anxiety can be debilitating and crippling, preventing us from leaving our house, while other times anxiety can be a nagging thought that makes it hard for us to sleep soundly.

Cast all your anxiety on him because he cares for you.

(1 Peter 5:7)

Anxiety wastes time and energy while distracting us from what matters most in our lives

Who of you by worrying can add a single hour to your life? Since you cannot do this very little thing, why do you worry about the rest?

(Luke 12:25–26)

It is hard not to be anxious when you consider that difficult things will happen to us. We will get sick, we will be disappointed, we will be hurt, and we will experience grief and loss. These are the facts of life. Worrying about such things doesn't change the fact: difficult things happen. And while this is all true, we aren't left to fight our anxiety on our own. Rather, God offers us immense promises and provisions that can allow us to live a life free of our anxieties.

> Then Jesus said to his disciples: "Therefore I tell you, do not worry about your life, what you will eat; or about your body, what you will wear.
>
> (Luke 12:22)

> Do not be anxious about anything, but in every situation, by prayer and petition, with thanksgiving, present your requests to God.
>
> (Philippians 4:6)

For instance, consider your finances or your health. Have you ever worried about money? Have you ever worried about how you will pay a bill, save for the future, or cover your needs? Have you ever worried that you would get sick? Have you ever worried that you or a loved one would end up with a fatal illness? Most of us can relate to that anxiety. But God promises to provide for us—just enough for each day. He promises us that He will turn our trouble into good—even sickness. His promise doesn't guarantee a trouble free life, or the how or the what of His plans and provision—He is the Creator of the universe—He can care for and provide for us however He pleases. It's simply up to us to keep our eyes on Him, trust His promise, receive with gratitude, and steward His gifts.

As we deepen our trust in Him, we begin to live a life more full of faith and less riddled by anxiety.

**Personal Reflection:**
- What role does anxiety play in your life?
- Has anxiety helped you? When has it harmed you?
- What promise can you hold onto the next time anxiety overwhelms you?
- What might your life look like if you lived with less worry?

**Prayer:**

God, I'm sorry for the ways that I worry and doubt your promises. Forgive me for wasting so much of my time obsessed with life's what-ifs. Help me to live by faith more deeply and give me peace to live out your plans for my life, even in troubling times. Help me to live more aligned with your promises.

# Day 23

Anger is a natural emotion. Even God burned with anger in the time of the Israelites. There are certain times for righteous anger. When we see others maltreated, when people we love betray us, or even as we sit back and watch the people in our culture being enticed to ways of thinking that take them further away from God's truth. Bringing this anger to God in prayer can help you to find peace as you keep your eyes on Him.

Sometimes we can be angry because a deep emotional need that we have is not being met by a loved one or was not met in childhood. No matter where our anger comes from, we are to be sure not to sin in our anger. It is important that we grow in becoming slow to anger.

"In your anger do not sin": Do not let the sun go down while you are still angry, and do not give the devil a foothold.

(Ephesians 4:26–27)

My dear brothers and sisters, take note of this: Everyone should be quick to listen, slow to speak and slow to become angry,

(James 1:19)

Sometimes we are angry for sinful reasons. Maybe you become easily offended or you didn't get your way, and instead of being disappointed and moving on, you hang onto anger and resentment. Maybe there was a miscommunication and you heard something that misrepresented the intention of a friend. Often when anger is for sinful reasons we become stuck in anger rather than seeking clarification, offering forgiveness and reaching a resolution.

The Bible says many things about forgiveness:

Be kind and compassionate to one another, forgiving each other, just as in Christ God forgave you.

(Ephesians 4:32)

Bear with each other and forgive one another if any of you has a grievance against someone. Forgive as the Lord forgave you.

(Colossians 3:13)

Even if they sin against you seven times in a day and seven times come back to you saying 'I repent,' you must forgive them."

(Luke 17:4)

When anger stems from sin, when anger causes sin, or when anger prevents us from living compassionately toward others, anger can act like a prison in which we are stuck. When anger evolves into resentment and we fail to forgive, we actually punish ourselves rather than the person with whom we are angry. This is often the case when we spin around negative thoughts and emotions. This type of thinking can be especially self-absorbed.

Our flesh often does not want to forgive. Because of the power of our anger and the way that Satan works to skew our thinking, we often fail to see that forgiveness actually delivers freedom. When we forgive, we experience a weight being lifted, and we allow room for greater grace, mercy, compassion, and love.

It is important to keep in the center of your perspective that we forgive because God first forgave us. God gave to us in abundance, and we are gifted with eternity alongside Him because of Jesus. In Jesus, we are forgiven, and we too are called to forgive.

**Personal Reflection:**
- Do you get angry easily? Would others describe you as an angry person?
- Are you holding onto bitterness or resentment? How does that impact your life?
- Do you practice forgiveness? Describe a time that you practiced forgiveness. What was the outcome?
- What step can you take today toward forgiving someone who has caused you pain?

**Prayer:**
God, forgive me for not forgiving others. Thank you for forgiving me. I need you to soften my heart and help me to love others as you have loved me. Help me in my unforgiveness. I want to live a life of freedom.

# Day 24

## Negative Thinking

To keep a Biblical perspective, we must think about what we are thinking about. It is so easy to be stuck in negative thinking.

Beyond the fact that negative thinking can greatly hinder our experience of a full and complete life, negative thinking is often part of Satan's plan to distract us from God's love and goodness. We may think that our negative thoughts are always a natural part of our experience as a human. But actually, our negative thoughts can be a result of Satan's scheme against us. This is why the Bible directs us to take our thoughts captive and make them obedient to Christ. This is how we battle the lies of Satan that permeate our perspective causing negative feelings, moods, and attitudes.

> We demolish arguments and every pretension that sets itself up against the knowledge of God, and we take captive every thought to make it obedient to Christ.
>
> (2 Corinthians 10:5)

> Do not conform to the pattern of this world, but be transformed by the renewing of your mind. Then you will be able to test and approve what God's will is—his good, pleasing and perfect will.
>
> (Romans 12:2)

Those who live according to the flesh have their minds set on what the flesh desires; but those who live in accordance with the Spirit have their minds set on what the Spirit desires. The mind governed by the flesh is death, but the mind governed by the Spirit is life and peace.

(Romans 8:5–6)

In short, God allows us control of our thoughts, and He commands us to align our thoughts with that of Jesus. That's a mighty command, but it is incredibly important. Our thoughts have great power in and of themselves. Our thoughts can dictate our lives, and I don't know about you, but I'd much rather be dictated by thoughts aligned with Jesus than thoughts influenced by Satan. When our negative thoughts consume us, our interactions, relationships, and circumstances begin to reflect the negativity in our minds.

The hardest part is that we often don't even identify our negative thoughts as negative, because the lies run so deep that they seem like realistic thoughts. Taking those thoughts captive, analyzing if it is in line with the Bible, and then changing it to be in obedience with the way that Christ instructs us to think is not an easy task.

Consider a gratitude practice, thanking God for even the seemingly insignificant things in your life. Spend time remembering what God has done for you, and allow those memories to encourage you as you move through this world. Read God's truths, and allow His love and goodness to seep into your mind. When you do, you will be surprised at the shift that occurs across every facet of your life.

**Personal Reflection:**
- Do you think about what you are thinking about?
- How often do you filter your thoughts through the truth of God's Word?
- What negative thought have you labeled as truth that does not match up with the way God instructs us to think?
- What is one truth from scripture you can pray to bring more positivity into your thought life?

**Prayer:**

God, Forgive me for my negative thinking. Help me to live more full of gratitude and remembrance of your goodness. Bring awareness of negative and untrue thoughts that I have labeled as truth and help me to change the way I think.

# Day 25

I have never met anyone who has escaped financial stress. Most of us have faced a situation where we did not know how we would get the money to pay for a financial need in our lives. Even the wealthy experience a burden to maintain their wealth whether it be by sustained income or savvy investments. The worry surrounding money is an experience to which everyone can relate. The Bible warns us not to allow money to become more important to us than our Lord.

> "No one can serve two masters. Either you will hate the one and love the other, or you will be devoted to the one and despise the other. You cannot serve both God and money.
>
> (Matthew 6:24)

> For where your treasure is, there your heart will be also.
>
> (Matthew 6:21)

The world values money and sees it as the foremost important way of providing for our families. The Bible tells us that God is our provider. Many times we struggle when we are called into a career that is paid lower than it should, or if we are called to leave a job that pays well to focus on the care of our family or to work in ministry. If you are following God's call then you are in the best place that you can be. You are building into the Kingdom and serving the Lord, even when it doesn't seem to make sense based on the values of culture. You are doing a great thing! God is our provider.

> Keep your lives free from the love of money and be content with what you have, because God has said, "Never will I leave you; never will I forsake you." So we say with confidence, "The Lord is my helper; I will not be afraid. What can mere mortals do to me?"
>
> (Hebrews 13:5–6)

God warns against the love of money, and He offers a special caution to those who are deemed rich. In short, God does not warn against wealth, but the slippery slope of seeking after wealth at the cost of our focus on Him. He is also clear about keeping our hope only in the Lord and not if we have a financial safety net. Only He is our safety net. Our focus is to be on Him.

> Command those who are rich in this present world not to be arrogant nor to put their hope in wealth, which is so uncertain, but to put their hope in God, who richly provides us with everything for our enjoyment. Command them to do good, to be rich in good deeds, and to be generous and willing to share. In this way they will lay up treasure for themselves as a firm foundation for the coming age, so that they may take hold of the life that is truly life.
>
> (1 Timothy 6:17–19)

It is crucial to examine your relationship with money. Are you generous? Do you save? God gives generously so that we might be conduits of His generosity, not so that we might be hoarders of His provisions. He promises to give to each of us richly according to the richness of His glory, not for our own comfort and ease.

I recommend spending some time praying through Matthew 25:14–30. This parable is metaphorical but also has application to how we are to see and manage money. What He does provide, if we spend it all, it will be gone. So we are to attempt to live within what He provides for us, even if that means we have to sacrifice certain comforts, possibly things that you think you need are not really that necessary or God wants you to go without for a time to grow you in your faith. God urges us to trust Him to provide for our financial needs. He cares for us more deeply than we can imagine, and because of His love, we can put our anxiety to rest.

**Personal Reflection:**
- Describe a time when the love of money caused you to make a poor decision.
- How is the accumulation of wealth a slippery slope to temptation?
- How are you a conduit of God's generosity?
- How is God providing for you financially?

**Prayer:**
Lord God, forgive me for my love of money. Lead me in generosity that I might more freely give out of the abundance you have given to me. Help me to foster a relationship with money that glorifies you and you alone.

# Day 26

## Negative Experiences

Life is full of traumas and negative experiences. Sometimes these things are accidents, and sometimes these things are due to our own sin or someone else's sin. Maybe these truths are still sinking in for you: difficult things will happen, pain and suffering are inevitable in life, and the Christian life is not synonymous with an easy street. And yet simultaneous to all that, God invites us to a life of joy, hope, love, compassion, and grace. Without Jesus, there is no living joyfully amidst the negativity of this world. But God provides a way. In fact, He provides the only way.

> The Lord is near to all who call on him, to all who call on
> him in truth. He fulfills the desires of those who fear him;
> he hears their cry and saves them.
>
> (Psalm 145:18–19)

Negative experiences are a part of living life on this earth. Some of us have known enough traumas and negative experiences to fill volumes of books while others of us have had negative experiences sprinkled throughout our lives. No matter your difficult experiences or lack thereof, there is hope! God promises to redeem all of it. The pain, the heartache, the sadness, the loss, and the grief—all of that is redeemable by God, and all of that has purpose in His kingdom. He can use that pain and heartbreak to help others to find Him. You can be used by the Lord for the most profound purpose of all: to grow His spiritual kingdom.

> The Lord is compassionate and gracious, slow to anger, abounding in love. He will not always accuse, nor will he harbor his anger forever; he does not treat us as our sins deserve or repay us according to our iniquities. For as high as the heavens are above the earth, so great is his love for those who fear him; as far as the east is from the west, so far has he removed our transgressions from us. As a father has compassion on his children, so the Lord has compassion on those who fear him;
>
> (Psalms 103:8–13)

Go to your Heavenly Father with your traumas and negative experiences. He will bring you out of the darkness and bring purpose to your pain. He will bind up the wounds and refresh you with His power.

When we allow ourselves to discover how God intersects with our negative experiences, we find a God of deep compassion, strength, and sovereignty. Experiencing this compassion and healing allows us to have a greater role in extending compassion to others, helping them to find their own healing in Christ. There is no greater purpose than that.

> Then they cried to the Lord in their trouble, and he saved them from their distress. He brought them out of darkness, the utter darkness, and broke away their chains. Let them give thanks to the Lord for his unfailing love and his

wonderful deeds for mankind, for he breaks down gates of bronze and cuts through bars of iron.

(Psalm 107:13–16)

Our negative experiences are not a place where we can stay. What I mean by that is this: If you are stuck in the negative experiences of your past—if you think about them often, constantly feel the pain deeply or react to them as if they are happening to you over and over, it is crucial that you seek help. A Christian counselor can help you get unstuck. Healing is readily available; you simply have to surrender and ask for help. God will bring healing to those who seek Him. God is our healer, and His healing presence is a gift to anyone who is available.

**Personal Reflection:**
- What traumas or negative experiences do you need to take to the Lord today?
- How has God redeemed the negative experiences of your past?
- Are you stuck in negative experiences? If so, have you considered seeking help to become unstuck?

**Prayer:**
God, thank you for your love and compassion for me. Help me to surrender my pain and negative memories to you. I don't want to live stuck anymore. I want to experience redemption. I want to move down a path of becoming unstuck. Help me. Thank you for being my healer. I need you now more than ever.

# Day 27

**DEPRESSION**

The mental health community has made great strides in understanding depression. This progress is especially encouraging when we consider that signs of depression can be traced all the way back to the stories we read in the Bible. Job's pain, loss, and depression was so deep that he had a death wish. David, who wrote the psalms, wrote many psalms which depicted depressed feelings. And while depression can be a significant indicator of a chemical imbalance and may be a medical issue, the Bible does offer us a valuable antidote to depression: keeping our eyes fixed on the Lord.

"Come to me, all you who are weary and burdened, and I will give you rest. Take my yoke upon you and learn from me, for I am gentle and humble in heart, and you will find rest for your souls. For my yoke is easy and my burden is light."

(Matthew 11:28–30)

Another way to put this is having an eternal perspective; a thought process that is fixed on the purpose God has given us in this temporary life while living with the hope of eternity with our creator. When we have this eternal perspective, we begin to move away from "navel gazing," the idea that we are so concerned with our own wellbeing, wants, needs, and shortcomings that we can't see beyond ourselves. When all we can see is ourselves, we fail to acknowledge the needs of others, and we fail to align our lives with God's purpose for us. As a result, we get depressed.

While understanding depression is not always this cut and dry, keeping our eyes fixed on the Lord is most certainly a significant contributor to our freedom from depressed thoughts and feelings. Consider some of your darker emotional moments. What was the world telling you that you should be concerned with in that time? Were you able to think of anything outside of your own pain, sadness, or negativity?

> Do not conform to the pattern of this world, but be transformed by the renewing of your mind. Then you will be able to test and approve what God's will is—his good, pleasing and perfect will.
>
> (Romans 12:2)

Now consider if you were to fix your eyes on the Lord and allow Him to renew your mind within that darkness. There is power in allowing the light of our creator to break through that darkness. There is hope through all dark times. Our Heavenly Father can and will turn all things, even depression, into a blessing, bringing you closer to Him than you have been before as you rely on His Spirit to push through depressed feelings. He will turn your feelings into something that He can use for His Kingdom. Your part is to stop looking only at yourself and start looking to Him. He has the ability to care for us and give us what we need.

And we know that in all things God works for the good of those who love him, who have been called according to his purpose.

(Romans 8:28)

'He will wipe every tear from their eyes. There will be no more death' or mourning or crying or pain, for the old order of things has passed away.'

(Revelation 21:4)

Now it should be said that some cases of depression are clinical and require clinical support from a Christian therapist. If you are experiencing prolonged symptoms of depression or thoughts of death, it's crucial that you seek help and support immediately. That being said, many of us suffer seasons and bouts of depression that can be remedied by a shift in our perspective. I encourage you to try on this perspective shift and see how the Lord delivers you.

**Personal Reflection:**
- What role has depression played in your life?
- In your own words, how does an eternal perspective help to break the chains of depression?
- What does it look like for you to fix your eyes on the Lord?
- Describe a time in your life when you leaned on God to help you overcome your depressed thoughts.

**Prayer:**
Lord, Help me to shift my perspective so that I stop focusing

only on myself. I want to see beyond myself. I want to fix my eyes on you, and I want to see the needs of those around me. Help me to move my thoughts away from myself and up to you so that I might experience more fullness and wholeness in life.

# Day 28

## Heart Change

We learn in 1 Samuel 16 that although man looks at others and notices outward appearance, the Lord looks at the heart. God judges us on our hearts. He sees beyond what anyone else can truly see: He sees our hearts. And consequently, He changes us, and our lives, through our hearts. Our perspectives are a matter of our hearts. You can try to change how you think and how you look at things but your perspective must change to change your heart. In Ezekiel 11, we learn that our hearts are often divided and they can be either hearts of stone or of flesh. Also, there are examples of people in the Bible who had hardened hearts.

> I will give them an undivided heart and put a new spirit in them; I will remove from them their heart of stone and give them a heart of flesh.
>
> (Ezekiel 11:19)

The most important reason for intentionally keeping a Biblical, eternal perspective is that it will bring about heart change. Consider this in Matthew:

> "Teacher, which is the greatest commandment in the Law?" Jesus replied: "'Love the Lord your God with all your heart and with all your soul and with all your mind.'

This is the first and greatest commandment. And the second is like it: 'Love your neighbor as yourself.' All the Law and the Prophets hang on these two commandments."

(Matthew 22:36–40)

Jesus didn't say that what matters is how we behave by doing x, y, and z. He didn't say that what most matters is that we follow descriptive rules, laws, and commandments. Rather Jesus said that what matters most is how we love—with our hearts.

Both in how we love God and others is an extension of what is in our hearts. Through heart change, we can change how we think and feel about God, ourselves, and others which in turn will change how we treat others. When our hearts are changed, we live more in line with the commandments of God. Living aligned with God happens when we allow God to change our hearts to be more like His. This alignment brings about personal growth, healing, joy, and peace.

**Personal Reflection:**
- How have you experienced a change of heart in your life because of Jesus?
- In what area of your life do you need to experience a change of heart?
- When you consider allowing God to change your heart, what hesitations do you have and why?

**Prayer:**
Lord, I confess: Sometimes it's easier for me to have rules and boundaries than it is for me to let you change my heart. But I know

that your ways are not my ways, and I know that what you have in store for me is far greater than I can imagine. Soften my heart. Change my life from the inside out.

# Day 29

## Joy In The Lord

Some of us come to Christ thinking that it is going to make us happier. Sometimes we interpret God's promises to mean that things shouldn't be difficult. Though the Bible does promise that joy in the Lord is a characteristic of a close relationship with the Lord, a common misconception is that joy and happiness are one in the same. In fact, they are different.

Though joy and happiness have some overlaps, their origins are unique. Happiness tends to be driven by circumstance and is ruled by emotion that is also connected to our perspective and our thinking habits. When something goes your way or you have a pleasant experience, you may feel happy. Joy, or more specifically Biblical joy, is founded in the knowing that you belong to God, He is sovereign over your life, and in all things, He remains faithful and good.

In other words, joy comes from the Lord. It is not driven by our circumstances. In fact, you can experience joy even during hardship, difficulty, pain, and suffering. But how? How can one experience joy and trials simultaneously? When we rest in the truth that we have an eternal purpose, when we fix our eyes on things above, and when we live for the glory of God, joy begins to take shape in our lives despite the terrible things going on around us, and to us.

> May the God of hope fill you with all joy and peace as you
> trust in him, so that you may overflow with hope by the
> power of the Holy Spirit.
>
> (Romans 15:13)

This is not to say that joy is putting on a happy face even when difficult things happen. Rather, when difficult things happen, we can sit in the pain, sadness, grief, loss, and disappointment with great hope and perseverance that stems from the understanding that this life is not our home, and one day every tear will be wiped from our face by the Almighty Creator. When we can look to God in our times of trials and pain, we will discover the peace of God, the steady of His hand, the love of a Father, the grace of His presence, and the calm of His friendship. In doing so, we find and know joy.

> So with you: Now is your time of grief, but I will see you
> again and you will rejoice, and no one will take away your
> joy.
>
> (John 16:22)

Although none of us want to go through difficult things, and we pray to avoid them, hardships and trials are opportunities to draw closer to the Lord. There are times in my life that, when I look back, I am thankful for the hardship because the joy that I now have in that area is because I learned to surrender my own plans and embrace the good that God could bring out of that hardship. Looking back on them, trials brought with them a confidence in God's sovereignty, and His supreme power and authority as I can look at the other side of it. As we seek to experience His peace, healing, and love, we find His beautiful, sincere, and intimate joy.

> Nehemiah said, "Go and enjoy choice food and sweet drinks, and send some to those who have nothing prepared. This day is holy to our Lord. Do not grieve, for the joy of the Lord is your strength."
>
> (Nehemiah 8:10)

If you are dealing with a trial today, have hope. Seek the Lord's comfort and purpose for allowing this trial in your life or the lives of your loved ones as you experience it together. Spend time in prayer and worship, focusing on His perfect will. Let His joy wash over you, and be renewed from the inside out.

**Personal Reflection:**
- In your own words, what is the difference between happiness and joy?
- Describe a time that you experienced joy despite the difficult situation surrounding you.
- How can you experience the joy of the Lord today?
- What role does joy play in your life?

**Prayer:**
Lord, Thank you for your joy. Help me to seek, find, and embrace your joy despite the pain and suffering I endure. Forgive me for focusing on circumstantial happiness rather than your everlasting and enduring joy. Fill my heart with your joy.

# Day 30

## INTENTIONALLY PRACTICING FAITH

This devotional book has taken you through many deep concepts with lots of self reflection. Continue to ask yourself reflection questions like these. As you grow and deepen your relationship with the Lord and practice intentionally keeping a Biblical perspective, you will learn to love Him more and more. The Lord delights in your knowing and loving Him. He delights in knowing His children.

> Jesus replied: "'Love the Lord your God with all your heart and with all your soul and with all your mind.' This is the first and greatest commandment. And the second is like it: 'Love your neighbor as yourself.' All the Law and the Prophets hang on these two commandments."
>
> (Matthew 22:37–40)

Have you ever considered what influence you are having on this world? If you were to watch your interactions with others from the outside, what would you see? Are you loving others as yourself? Are you exemplifying the love of Jesus? Are you showing gratitude for the blessings you have? Does your attitude bring glory to God?

There is another purpose to our knowing and loving God. As we deepen our relationship with God, we can pass along a Biblical perspective to others. Your perspective and your attitude towards life, the world, others, and God will be contagious to your family, your friends, and your coworkers. Keeping a Biblical perspective with our eternal purpose at the center will change your thinking, your mood, and your attitude in life, bringing glory to God. It will change your life and everything that you do. This is what it means to give glory to God in all things.

> As iron sharpens iron, so one person sharpens another.
>
> (Proverbs 27:17)

A Biblical perspective is a gift not only for you, but also others because it provides them with an opportunity to know and love God. When we point to Jesus and set a good example of who Jesus is, we give God the credit for our lives while also giving others the opportunity to have the gift of faith.

Beyond deepening your own relationship with God, the faith you demonstrate is an encouragement to others. Encouraging others will bring you life. The more we can focus on the Lord and point others to Him, the more you will be filled with peace in your circumstances, purpose for your tasks, and joy even in the mundane. By living intentionally, loving your neighbor as yourself, serving others, and giving generously, you bring God glory, influence the world in grace, and point people to Jesus through your life.

> so we cared for you. Because we loved you so much, we were delighted to share with you not only the gospel of God but our lives as well.
>
> (1 Thessalonians 2:8)

Be intentional in your time with others. Work to be a positive influence and not a negative one. Through your example, encourage others to think positively and make a positive difference in this world instead of being self-focused like the rest of the world.

**Personal Reflection:**
- How do you practice your faith in your daily life? Are you deepening your relationship with the Lord?
- How do you love God with your whole heart, soul and mind?
- How do you love your neighbor as yourself?
- How can you be more intentional in your circumstances to practice your faith in your alone time and in your relationships with others?

**Prayer:**
I love you, Lord. I want to know you better. I want to deepen my relationship with you. Lead me in learning you. Help me to love you with my whole heart, mind and soul. Help me to love my neighbor as myself. I want to glorify you with my entire life. Thank you for grace.

# Day 31

## REMEMBERING GOD'S TRUTHS

When I started to homeschool my kids, a lesson that I had vaguely grasped in my own life was illuminated as a circumstance of humanity. In order for us to remember something that we have learned, we sometimes have to review that same lesson over and over again. Before homeschooling, our kids would come home from school and just know things. Once I was the teacher, I realized that even simple lessons had to be reviewed over and over and over again for them to really learn it.

I used to get frustrated with myself when God would teach me a lesson through a trial or painful battle in my life, and then a bit later I would forget what I learned. I didn't even realize it until I was in the middle of the same painful battle again. Then I would see that it is the same truth I learned last time.

For example, so many times I have had to learn to trust God with our finances. Over and over again when little things came up, I would be thrown back into anxiously thinking that I had to figure it out, and with it came all the what ifs. Feelings of scarcity would take over my emotions. Time and time again as I got myself all wound up because the weight felt too heavy, God would remind me that He is in control. I would then get frustrated with myself for allowing the ordeal because I had forgotten the truths that God brought me to last time money stress came up. But I have now learned that it is human to need to be reminded of things and to need to review the same lessons over again to really learn it.

My son, do not forget my teaching, but keep my commands in your heart,

(Proverbs 3:1)

There are times when a lesson we have learned is so impactful that we will never forget it, but there are also times when we have to learn that same lesson over and over again before it can break through our sinful thinking and habits.

As we learned previously in this devotional, the spiritual battle that we are in is a reality, and Satan wants us to forget. You may have heard the analogy that living the Christian life is like a fish swimming upstream. There is some reality in that picture. If we stop pursuing God's truth, the lies of the world will take aim at us and we will struggle in our journey.

Talking about the truths we have learned will keep it on our lips, and daily devotion and prayer time will help us to meditate on it regularly. That is how we will remember and will find victory over our trials, and negative thinking and emotions.

**Personal Reflection:**
- Look over days 1–10 of this devotional. List three things that you don't want to forget.
- Look over days 11–20 of this devotional. List three things that you don't want to forget.
- Look over days 21–30 of this devotional. List three things that you don't want to forget.

**Prayer:**

Father God, thank you for the journey we have taken together. Thank you for your love and for continually teaching me. Please help me to hold on to your truth as I swim upstream against culture. Transform my thoughts and renew my mind. Help me to become more like Jesus one lesson at a time.